Hipp

Contents

What Do Hippos Look Like?   2

Where Do Hippos Live?   6

What Do Hippos Eat?   8

What Do Hippos Do?   10

Index   16

What Do Hippos Look Like?

Hippopotamuses are big animals. They have thick skin. They have short legs. They have big teeth.

Big teeth

Short legs

Thick skin

Little ears

Little eyes

3

Hippos cannot
see well, but they
can smell well.
They can hear well.
They can run fast, too!

4

Where Do Hippos Live?

Hippos live
in Africa.
They live near
rivers and lakes.
They live with
other hippos.

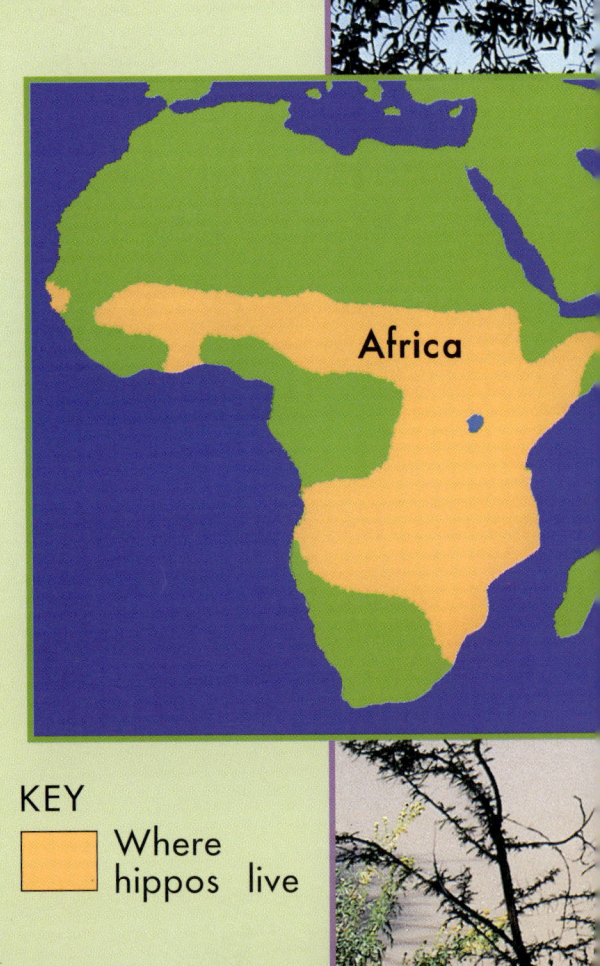

Africa

KEY

Where
hippos live

6

What Do Hippos Eat?

Hippos eat grass and other plants.

8

What Do Hippos Do?

Hippos like to swim. They can stay under the water for a long time. They like mud, too.

Mother hippos
look after their babies well.
They feed them milk.
They teach them to swim.

12

Hippos yawn
a lot.
This can mean,
"Keep away
from me!"

Index

Africa 6
babies 12
ears 3, 4
eyes 3, 4
food 8, 12
legs 2–3, 4
mud 10
skin 2–3
swimming 10, 12
teeth 2
water 6, 10, 12
yawning 14